Inside Anonymous Hacker Group

Dr. Donald JG Chiarella, CISM, CDMP, PEM, CHS-CIA

Hanover, Maryland 21076

May 2013

Inside Anonymous Hacker Group

Inside Anonymous Hacker Group

Table of Contents

Inside Anonymous Hacker Group

Inside Anonymous Hacker Group

Introduction

When I met the FBI Special Agent I was apprehensive. I did not know why he wanted to meet with me. He soon gave me a chance to help the FBI with infiltrating the hackers Anonymous. I only asked for a security clearance - no money. The agent was nice and personable. His experience and mine were miles apart. I decided I would like working for this man. He delegated me to his first agent and we met at the same Deli for lunch. He asked more questions about my background and gave me his email to get hold of him with any information I could find online. When I got back to the office I documented the conversations. I was now working part time for the FBI which I considered an honor. I had worked at the FBI Headquarters earlier in my career on the Headquarters Index System which was later replaced by the Name Check System.

What I found was my opinion about the group changed after studying them for 4 weeks. The idea of holding governments and corporations accountable has merit. But the means with which they perform this is not acceptable. I understand they feel powerless to control their lives. But they must find better ways to express their feelings rather than cyber attacks. Cyber attacks can lead to all out conventional warfare. We know this for sure. Not many civilians are ready to take up the mantle of freedom through arms. This is the military job description. And they are ramping up their cyber defenses every year. Most important I found more information on our cyber defenses than I expected. I was able to learn what major DOD systems were programmed in. Changing source code on the B-2. Jovial software is a matter of national security. We must protect these resources.

This report is what I found on Anonymous from the inside learning more each day and becoming a part of the organization .

Inside Anonymous Hacker Group

Chapter 1. Group definition

Anonymous is a decentralized hacker group of self taught computer people. They have learned to hack into computer websites and other servers and take what they want for private gain. They say they are for the common man in America yet they violate federal laws doing this to make political points. They say they are not political yet they make attacks on political computer assets. They recruit people from the ranks of the disgruntled citizens who have computer networking skills. They never see each other. They produce video tapes of important missions. Since they are decentralized they say they have no leader. Yet, Commander X seems to speak for the group often enough. Others speak for the group regularly in videos like mmawildal and Dave Gunslinger. These anonymous names are very hard to track.

It is clear that many anonymous group members have no hacking abilities at all and hire others to do this for them. This was verified in the News website where people tried to hire others to hack for them. The hacking intentions are then transferred to others in the group. Some members wanted to be trained. Others preferred to pay small sums of money $100-200 for each breech of a computer. The tasks ranged from changing grades to wiping out bills electronically. Many of the tasks were not of a larger political nature. The fear is that these small tasks could escalate into larger attacks on government and corporate websites and databases.

Inside Anonymous Hacker Group

Chapter 2. Group purpose

The Anonymous group purpose is to act as a social conscience for the people of America. They do this by attacking banks, government, celebrities, North Korea, and others who they think have wronged the people. They believe all government is corrupted. They may use a DDOS attack on websites. They may enter a website and change information on it. They have the means to steal millions of dollars though they say this is not their purpose. They also say they are not a terrorist group.

That depends on your definition of cyber terrorists. They certainly have the power and knowledge to commit these types of computer acts. Every few days a new video appears stating a new target and operation like a military service. They even have a group called Intelligence named Paranoia.

They may seem harmless but the very acts they commit are illegal and federal privacy laws are broken by them all the time. They probably have many younger people with computer skills and people who are not professional computer people. Most of them are self taught. It is not clear how detailed their knowledge of hacking and computer security goes. I do not think they can manufacture a virus or Trojan but that would not surprise me.

For the most part they are angry individuals who need attention. They abuse their freedoms and intrude in computers systems where they are not wanted. They do not deserve to die but they actually think they are performing service to the people of the USA.

Inside Anonymous Hacker Group

They hide behind the Guy Fawkes mask. He was a terrorist who bombed Parliament because he thought the government was corrupt. The movie "V for Vendetta" is a take off of this theme. Justice by the people for the people in a Democracy. While the idea is good the means are illegal. We vote for those who will lead us. This is our Democratic mechanism for change not violence.

Chapter 3. How to become Anonymous

You can become anonymous just by agreeing with their policies and actions. They never meet in public and never know each other. They do have rallies and protests together where they will wear their masks. If you buy a mask then you have become a member. If you watch videos and participate in hacking operations then you are a member. You are not secret and you are leaving electronic forensic trails. You can be tracked by IP address. You can be unmasked in public places.

The spirit of anonymous is one of independence and strength. I agree with the idea of having checks and balances on government. I do not agree with illegal hacking to accomplish this. I spent a major portion of my life learning computer programming skills to make a living. This group has hijacked those skills and made them something terrible to fear. A once peaceful software engineering career now involves cyber warfare methods of attacking enemies. This is the world we live in. To know the methods is to have unmitigated powers over legitimate software makers and the organizations they represent. It has created a new business of cyber security.

Anonymous membership will require you to either hack into company and personal websites or make video claims of this. You will be asked to hack into websites and databases illegally to get your results and post them online. You will not be given any budget or money to do this. You will not be given legal protection by any lawyers although they do have lawyers who represent them. You will be on your own never knowing who to trust. The criminal activities you may be asked to do are beyond most of us.

Inside Anonymous Hacker Group

http://anonnews.org/static/faq

I found the above website when i was searching for Anonymous members. This website has forums with all the data you need to become Anonymous. The vast majority of people on the news website do not have hacking skills. Many of them are looking for someone with these skills. The website is one of ideas to stop corruption and greed. Many people have ideas of how to take actions to stop corruption. Few if any of the people give their real names. They stay in the shadows. There are debates on the news website and announcements. It is an attempt to organize chaos. The website owner may have some deeper insights into the group. There appears to be a lot of teenagers and students on the website without any links to other groups in their life. Anger may play a part in joining.

Chapter 4. Hacking skills

Many hackers are self taught. Sometimes a good programmer will go to the dark side. There are many places now teaching hacking skills. SANS Institute is the best place. The DHS SENTINEL Program was another place hacking methods were taught to the computer forensic experts who protect systems. So the skills are available for the taking. It is not hard to learn network monitoring and sniffing. A brief time with Wireshark will get you up to speed on that. Wireshark is available online for free on internet. NETTOOLS 5 is another hacking toolset I have used in the past that is rather effective. The hacking skills include programming skills and scripting skills. To change source code on the fly and replace it where you found it is very dangerous. Replacing object code and modifying it in a DLL is even more dangerous but it can be done if you know hexadecimal and literals in object code. The right object code editor is all you need. You can find embedded passwords and all types of banners, headers, etc. This is how a majority of illegal software changes are done.

The types of attacks such as Distributed Denial of Service, SQL Injection, Man in the Middle, Phishing, Trojans, Viruses, and Malware are all directed by the machines of the attackers . These machines may control other machines called BOTNETS. The FBI has targeted BOTNETS across the country for many years in Operation BOTNET ROAST. The skills required to do these attacks are deviant and not normal for most programmers. A legitimate programmer knows he can make money programming regular source code. He does not need to hack.

With that said there are hackers who are called White Hat Hackers or CEH – Certified Ethical Hackers. Then there are hackers who are Black Hat. They meet annually at a Black Hat conference. They exchange methods and information and learn new hacking skills. White Hat hackers inform companies of security vulnerabilities in their software after testing. Not all hackers are bad.

Colleges teaching computer security assume some knowledge of programming. They also teach ethics to go with the security lessons. They have been expanding in recent years and may do a background check on students. I would assume that a certain percentage of these students could go bad and use their hacking skills for deviant purposes.

Chapter 5. Videos

Anonymous videos are well choreographed. Almost all of them have a male voice speaking. All of them have an image of an anonymous member in a mask at a desk. The videos come out at a rate of 1-2 a week on various subjects. They are not regulated. Anyone in the group can make one. There are discussions on what topics they will do. Members do talk to one another. Voice recognition software could be key here for investigations.

One video had a man with a tattoo on his right arm. Not smart to wear a mask and not cover up the identifying tattoo. The videos have news videos embedded in them. This suggests they are using high end video equipment to edit film. Almost all the videos follow the same pattern. Identification then discussion of actions by governments or companies or people in power. The voice on the video may not be of the actor in video wearing the mask. The videos usually end with a statement of who they are and what they believe.

WE ARE ANONYMOUS. WE ARE LEGION. WE DO NOT FORGIVE. WE DO NOT FORGET. EXPECT US.

After analyzing 4 years of videos I can tell you they are mostly the same taking credit for hacktivism where they may. One video even denied any involvement in the Boston Bombing. They seem to have a reverence for the military although they criticize them plenty and they have hacked the Pentagon. They do not seem to want to be labeled "Domestic Terrorists" yet their actions are not legal computer work. They have no idea that NATO has declared cyber terrorists can be killed.

Inside Anonymous Hacker Group

One video in London showed them walking to a protest with their masks on and talking to the London Police who asked them to take off their masks. One of them complied and complained. The rest of them did not comply. The officers did not arrest them. They laughed about the fact that they were able to talk their way out of an arrest.

Another video shows President Obama making speeches during his campaigns. They attack his policies on gun control and the use of Sandy Hook people to help make policy. They show no preference for either party in Congress. They do not seem capable of running for Congress which has never had a computer scientist elected. This is the logical approach to lasting change by the group but they seem to not be capable of this thinking.

I am still waiting on the video to change the government through voting for a candidate who is an Anonymous member. This will be the evolution of the group into political power. This can be done similar to the Tea Party candidates. I would suspect they are thinking about this seriously. They would probably get a high percentage of the votes from the 99%. The problem is that this candidate would then be changed by the political system and not be able to deliver on his promises due to majority rules.

This idea has merit though and is a peaceful way for Anonymous to obtain legitimate power.

Inside Anonymous Hacker Group

Chapter 6. FBI

The FBI has many good computer people. I worked there in 1990 for 4 months and met some good staff members. They have the latest in technology – mainframes and networks. Their labs are the best in the world at ballistics, finger printing, facial recognition, voice prints, palm prints, and retinal scans. They are working on other secure biometrics with NIST.

The FBI may be the one place that computer scientists are welcomed in the federal government besides NSA. Many support jobs involve computers. They just fielded the SENTINEL system of case management inside the FBI. This promises to make processing cases easier. The Justice Data Processing Center in West Virginia has plenty more offsite computing power. If I were Anonymous I would not underestimate the people at the FBI. They are very professional and very well educated. Many of them ex-Military and very motivated.

The FBI is poised to take back control of American networks and internet. They have dedicated themselves to making sure no group disrupts the internet. The Internet Crime Center is located at the FBI website. Citizens can complain about crimes there. The bigger picture is to develop a cybercrime capability that can stop and capture white collar crime in action. Cybercrime and white collar crime are often linked together like fraud and counterfeiting. Organized crime can use computers too. The FBI is there to say "No" to all of these.

Fidelity, Bravery, & Integrity (FBI Motto on statue at Headquarters) will live on as long as the USA is a free country. We all need to take time to help them do their jobs.

Infragard has many members who do not help the FBI. This needs to change.

Information needs to flow both ways in the Infragard groups.

Chapter 7. Protests – 99%

Protests are an American institution since the 1960s. Meaningful change was the result of Nixon's response to US protests over Vietnam. He ended the draft and the Vietnam War because of protests. They usually work wonders when they are peaceful. Civil rights protests had their impact on lawmakers. The protests in the Arab nations has been a pathway of change in those countries. In a way Anonymous is based on the protest principle. Only the protest is ongoing and never ending. It actually represents anarchy if there is always a protest. The 99% protest featured many members of Anonymous wearing their masks to the rallies. This is a good way to indentify the members of the group. I would suggest that public mask wearing will become a way to the jail cell.

Protests against the 1% are effective unless the 1% are those in power which is the case in America. The top 1% of income run the country and the world. These people are the builder bergers, trilateral commission, and illuminati. They have long wanted a new world order of one government. The 1% may have some good people but they mostly do what is right for themselves not others. Some politicians pretend to be 99% supporters but this is false. Those same politicians are millionaires with no income problems at all living in the 1%. The founding fathers did not want congress to become a millionaires club but it has. They are part of the 1% and they will never give up power once they have it. Term limits (2 terms for all) are required to bring us back to regular people running the country. George Washington would approve. He rejected kinghood when it was offered to him. And he was a very moral man – a Master Mason and Worshipful Master of Alexandria Lodge. No other president has lived up to him yet.

In current money he was worth $512 million dollars - the richest ever. Washington set a high standard for all American presidents. Jefferson was an Illuminati but not a Mason. Truman was also a Worshipful Master of the Missouri Lodge. The Masonic Lodge is the prototype for congressional voting and the democratic process. The power is in the participation of all required to vote on major business.

Chapter 8. Masks

The Guy Fawkes mask is not a good idea. First it identifies who you are. Second when you buy it the store remembers who bought it. If the FBI rounded up all the people who bought a mask they would have most of the Anonymous on trial. My first plan was to purchase a mask and infiltrate the crowd at the next protest. Then I realized that was not even required. I bet the FBI has the names of those who purchased masks and is monitoring them right now. You basically blew it by needing a mask to signify your allegiance. I prefer a Baltimore Orioles hat.

Wearing a Guy Fawkes mask means you agree with terrorism. If you do not want to be called a Domestic Terrorist then do not wear a terrorist's mask. This is a simple logic. By wearing this man's mask you are agreeing with a Domestic Terrorism agenda. This cannot be tolerated by any of the developed countries since we have democratic elected officials.

Chapter 9. Networking

Networking in Anonymous is basically not allowed. The best you can do is videos to keep up with the antics of the few who are active hackers and the news website. I suspect a few are actually doing the damage to the corporate websites and North Korea and others. I did not find these persons during my time looking for them. I would need more powerful tools to capture data indicating whom was doing the hacking from what IP addresses. The FBI has these tools as I understand and they will have watched many suspects by now. The people on the news website had a number of things to say about Anonymous. Some were recruiting hackers – others were announcing major operations. Some were debating with non Anonymous people.

I found other hacking groups who told Anonymous they would put them out of business. One even did a video on the topic and said they were more powerful than anonymous and they could shut down anonymous websites and hacking abilities. This group was S3curity. Another hacking group claimed the same thing.

I would suppose the FBI is interested in hackers against hackers. Another group is just as hard to track as Anonymous. But it benefits everyone if Anonymous is shut down by all of us law abiding citizens.

If the congress taxes internet then Anonymous would be violating IRS tax laws by their intrusion on the internet. This could change the federal charges against members of Anonymous network of hackers.

The Anonymous News website is the official place to network with other members of Anonymous. This website allows members to discuss plans in forums and IRC Chat sessions. The planning function of Anonymous is done here. Hackers are hired and tasks assigned for the cause. The tasks may be small or big. Operation level tasks are kept as secret as possible.

Chapter 10. Staying Anonymous

If you are planning on staying Anonymous do not do a video. Once you do a video the FBI has your voice track, height, weight and any features you show on the video. Do you really think they do not trace phone calls and can not match your voice patterns? The FBI has techniques that no other police force has. You are underestimating them grossly. The best way to stay anonymous is to never go to rallies and never communicate with anyone. After all you can not communicate with them all unless you are producing videos. The FBI can not read your mind. If you are decentralized from everyone and you have your belief system then you better just stick to that. Your desire to spread the gospel to the rest of us will get you caught. Your computer skills will also get you caught if you are not careful. The evidence on your computer will be used against you in court when you are captured. Whatever you erase will be recovered by FBI cybercrime forensics analysts. It is a no win situation to be Anonymous these days. Remember who you talk to and who you discuss these matters with. They might be FBI informants. Do not even share an email with someone or that could be used against you too.

The anonymous entries at the news website are not tracked to my knowledge but that does not mean they can not be. The FBI has powerful tools to track down who they want by IP address.

Chapter 11. Infiltrating Anonymous

In 4 weeks I was able to infiltrate Anonymous and find targets in DOD for source code on major weapons systems. I was never caught and I always watched the videos. I passed this information to the FBI agents. I suspect they already had much of what I sent them. I never bought a mask. Did not want to be tracked by credit card. I did notice who was sending what videos. I did not try to contact them nor attend any protests. Protests are not my thing. I prefer secret voting in the Masonic Lodge on business issues. I think that I could have tried to meet some people in Anonymous with comments of the websites but that would have been too obvious. The quandary is how do you catch people who are wearing masks that others are wearing who may or may not have committed crimes? In America you need hard evidence.

I found the Anonymous News website and it showed me how they are meeting online and setting up the operations they are doing. This website is located at http://anonnews.org/static/faq.

The best thing to do would be to login and track some of the conversations and discussions. I did this for several hours. I came to understand why they meet online to stay anonymous. I even had some remarks of my own which I did not enter about Freemasons and the Illuminati not being the same group. I am a Freemason and I have not met any Illuminati.

I felt like I could have believed in some of the things they said in their videos but I would not do any hacking. I also think that it is ok to think the government is corrupt because some of it really is corrupt! But on a far less scope than you think. Individual people become corrupt with power given to them by the system. Rooting out these people is far harder than attacking a website. I know I have been a whistleblower for more than 20 years inside my agencies. I was driven by senior managers and executives who thought nothing of promoting people they liked over others who earned it. "Yes" men never appealed to me. I lost 2 jobs because I spoke my mind about poor leadership. Once you get over that you can always find other ways to speak out. Anonymous may be one way for some people who want to keep their day jobs. Our system has come to this point in time. If we are not careful a total police state will ensue. President Eisenhower said to be careful about the military industrial complex running America. I say we live in a time when a Police State is justified by our leaders every time the terrorist bell rings. This is not wise. One day the switch will go "on" and stay "on" like in Nazi Germany. Civil liberties are worth protecting according to FBI Director Mueller.

Chapter 12. Jail Time

Jail time is deterrent to many crimes. No one wants to go to jail for a cyber crime. This is becoming more and more prevalent these days as judges impose stricter sentences on cyber criminals. I do not expect the death sentence to be imposed but there is movement towards this in NATO who says that cyber crime deserves death to the cyber criminal who starts a cyber war. I suspect cyber crooks do not like jail time either because it isolates them from the computer networks and because they can not make any money from their crime.

It is not clear if people logging into the news website forum is illegal. It would be problematic once they decide to use it as a connector for illegal activities. Jail time should be a deterrent but many of these people are just teenagers or frustrated people with the systems of America.

Chapter 13. Privacy Act violations

As a DBA you pledge to protect your databases privacy according to the Privacy Act of 1974 and the Electronic Privacy Act. You never give out data to anyone who does not have authorization to see it. You protect personal information and addresses. Yet many companies sell this information for advertising purposes. This really violates the spirit of the law. How would you like a company to sell your online data to someone? It has probably already been done without your consent or knowledge.

This privacy would extend to the ISP companies. They are giving the FBI everything they have on customers or they face federal charges. This means your every move online is tracked by the FBI. Every website you visit and every URL you type in is tracked for the world to see. So you should expect no Privacy in the USA either from companies or the FBI.

Anonymous is violating the privacy act every time they hack into a computer. Someday the penalty for this crime will be big enough to make a difference. Anonymous will be held accountable for privacy invasions by judges during sentencing. Those helping the attackers violate the privacy act will also be held accountable.

How do you prevent Privacy Act violations? Increase layered security. James Martin called this the security onion. You add physical security, procedural security, environmental security, encryption, and better password security. Today you also add multi variable authentication and SSL protection. The more security you put on the network the better you will protect the Privacy Act. Security people know about layered defenses. They also know about Defense in Depth or the idea that more security layers is better.

The DBA knows about security also and he has a responsibility to ensure his databases use encryption and other methods of hiding passwords and critical security data. This is basic DBA 101. Application Programmers may not be as familiar with how to encrypt data and passwords but the DBA and Lead Systems Programmer or Network Administrator are definitely in the loop on this.

Chapter 14. Leaders

Anonymous leaders emerge from the videos and protests. Those willing to talk to the press are also high profile. Commander-X was one who did not claim to be a leader but always popped up during my time researching them. The group claims to be leaderless. Yet often operations come from the same screen names like mmawildal in videos. This suggests that leaders have merged from the group even though they state they have no leaders. Inside the Anonymous network they can trust no one due to high infiltration by the authorities.

The Anonymous News website is where they meet online. http://anonnews.org/static/faq This is the best place to find more detailed information on operations and recruiters of hackers. There are plenty of forums with discussions that are clandestine in nature. They claim that Anonymous is an idea not a group. It is obvious that the leaders are using this website to do their business. I would watch this website from a secure location and trace various names. I attempted to predict where Operation USA would end up going and did not find anything directly related to it. Maybe the best way to follow these things is to have special agents read the news daily to determine where they are planning their next attacks. This website is clearly helpful with that objective.

Inside Anonymous Hacker Group

Chapter 15. Ethical Hacking

Ethical hacking is when a person is trying to help stop regular hacking. The certified ethical hacker can be a policeman or anyone wearing a white hat. This person will teach hacking methods to others and become a force against hacking. Anonymous is not ethical hacking. They have confused the meaning and taken on the moniker of evil acts of hacking. This is highly illegal and laws will have to evolve to place these people under arrest.   They hide behind the Anonymous computer names. Anonymous News website tries to make the case that they are ethical hackers. This is not the truth. These hackers are hired for illegal works by people with criminal intents. The hackers with real skills need to beware that they do not end up in an illegal activity on the Anonymous News website.

Chapter 16. Democracy or Domestic Cyber Terrorists

Is Anonymous Democracy in action or is it Domestic Cyber Terrorism? I would have to say that the activities of the hackers are illegal in nature and law. They are criminals if they decide to work for someone on the Anonymous website. The actions of terrorism are violent. Anonymous tries to stay away from violent activities. The actions they take to invade computer privacy could trigger violence.This then would lead to cyber terrorism. Digital crime is still crime. The types of digital fraud and crime can be huge. It goes way beyond simple DDOS attacks.

Democracy is where people are allowed to be represented and speak out on issues of the day. Anonymous does have a component that allows for freedom of speech on the computer. But when hacking is involved the speech is more like criminal actions. Computer democracy is anonymous when people give their true opinions. This idea has merit but it is being hijacked by the criminal component of the people to do harm on the computer. Anonymous as an idea is a good way to give opinions. Political offices frequently use survey research to obtain opinions. Anonymous opinions are more of an outcry from the public who use computers and wish to stay secret. If Anonymous runs an elected official as a group then they are entering the representative Democracy properly.

Inside Anonymous Hacker Group

Chapter 17. My Professional Views

The idea of Anonymous has merit as an opinion generator of computer users. It goes awry when hackers are being hired to do illegal activities. As a computer science college instructor I would never teach my students how to hack a network. SANS Institute has a hacking course that teaches that. It is no longer a closed secret and the skills can be obtained in one semester. Cyber security colleges have the power to create ethical hackers who can stop this poor behavior of criminal hackers.

The absolute worse hacker would be the one who hacks into the DOD systems and makes changes to their software source code and exits. This hacker has extreme skills in languages and network hacking. The law enforcement staffer may have a hard time tracking this guy. Modern law enforcement draws on students of cyber security schools too. These students are smart enough to help find and prosecute the black hats.

Chapter 18. Politics of Anonymous

The politics of anonymous are amorphous of all the views held by members of the group. There is not one defined party for the group. In fact, they are more anarchist than anything else. In this regard they are anti-government claiming to be against general corruption. If this is the case then they also claim to act as the conscience of the people. This is true of most anarchists. They fail to run for elected office because they do not believe in the very system they are trying to topple. It is a noble cause to hold governments accountable. It is quite a different story to destroy them with computer hacking skills. Privacy of the individual suffers in the process. There is no online privacy anymore. One could look at Anonymous as the perpetual whistleblower. This task requires total absolution from retaliation. It also demands an anti establishment attitude that pervades future actions.

Peaceful revolutions use the petition system allowed in the government. Anonymous leads to criminal hacking activities that try to capitalize on the vast lack of laws in the internet world. Future laws could be made much more tough to deal with Anonymous. Congress just does not have enough information at this point – none of them are computer scientists. But there is hope for the future where computer people can make policy. It will not be the hackers making this policy. Anonymous is bottom up leadership and this can have value at times. But it prevents the group from being represented in Congress. It would be wiser to run elected officials who can change the system from inside.

Chapter 19. Conclusions

We have looked at the intents of Anonymous. We have infiltrated the group and viewed intelligence websites and news websites from inside Anonymous. There is nothing remarkable about this group. It is a loosely controlled group of computer users who are trying to impact policy through hacking computers. The group would be far more empowered if they ran for elected office such as the Tea Party did. If they are truly an idea with merit then they would give up illegal hacking and try the honest way to influence politics. But they basically say there is no honest way to influence politics in America for the little guy. This is just not true. If you have the right connections online you can sign petitions, send congress letters, and give small donations to various good causes. This is the honest way to influence power. It does not come by hacking into any website and violating the Privacy Act.

Chapter 20. Bibliography

http://anonnews.org/static/faq

Chiarella, Donald (2012), Digital Crime and Forensics, Lulu Press, Research Triangle , NC.

Chiarella, Donald (2012), Digital Money, Lulu Press, Research Triangle, NC.

Chiarella, Donald (2011), Modern CyberWarfare: Bulletproof Systems, Lulu Press, Research Triangle, NC.

Chapter 21. Biography

Donald Chiarella is a Homeland Security Coordinator in Maryland DOT. He has expertise on cybersecurity, emergency management, and transportation security. He consults with other agencies and law enforcement such as Maryland State Police and the FBI. Don is a retired federal IRM manager (GM-13). He also worked for Navy Medical for 10 years as a Computer Specialist (GS-12) and was in the Air Force as a cadet at USAFA in 1974-5. Don attended Naval Post Graduate School, GWU, Ashford University, American University, University of Maryland, DODCI, and NIH DCRT. He holds a PhD in MIS, an MS in Technology Mgt, a BA in Org Mgt, and a BA in Urban Studies and IFSM. He has taken FEMA training in Emergency Mgt and Cyber security. He was also part time computer sciences professor. Don has written 25 books available at www.lulu.com/donchiarella.